FIRECLAY

Munia Khan

ISBN 978-1-950818-65-5 (paperback)

Copyright © 2020 by Munia Khan

All rights reserved. No part of this publication may be reproduced, distributed, or transmitted in any form or by any means, including photocopying, recording, or other electronic or mechanical methods without the prior written permission of the publisher. For permission requests, solicit the publisher via the address below.

Rushmore Press LLC
1 888 733 9607
www.rushmorepress.com

Printed in the United States of America

Contents

Preface 9
Acknowledgements 11

Reflected Stance 13
Fireclay 13
Along the Shore 14
Altered 15
Dream Revamped 15
Near a Lighthouse 17
Deceitful 17
Hollow Deeds 17
Stars Between 18
Sailing Love 18
Eagle's Flight 19
Trees 19
Riddle's Death 20
Predicament 20
Towards the Waves 20
Never Allow 21
Being Empty 21
Mutual Friends 21
To Feel A Tranquil Life 22
City Night 22
Abode 22
Vincible 23
Rejoice 23
Sleepless Soul 24
Unharboured 24

Shadows of Clouds	24
Startled	25
When You Feel Sad	25
My Musing	25
From the Diary of An Old Train	26
Misled	28
Lightning And Rainbow	28
Pelican	28
From Another World	29
To Zaima: My Daughter	32
New Year's Eve	33
Taste of Your Words	33
Empty Winds	34
Hold My Hand	34
Candlelit love	34
When You Are Gone	35
Armored	35
Palestine	36
Atonement	36
Mingling With the Green	36
Poor Dear Piano	37
Wilted And Empty	38
Remembrance	38
Raindrop	38
We Can Never Tell	39
Into the Bonfire	39
Electronic	40
Never an Unborn	40
Create Your World	42
Summer 2018	43
Mortality's Song	43
Peacefully Tanned	43
Apart	44
If I Were	44
Adieu to My Twisted Being	45
How You Love Me	46

Truth	46
From the Passionate Vine	47
Everything You Are	48
To the Wise Cupid	49
Deceiver	50
Tiny Abode	51
To the Queen of Trees (Part I)	51
To the Queen of Trees (Part – II)	52
Just To Swing	52
Through the Verse of Blood	53
Afterlife	53
Listen Hard	54
Shark	54
A Pair of Love Poems	54
Rhyme From an Insomniac	55
In Love with Memories	55
The Dying One	56
On Your Birthday	57
Word-Power	57
Under My Skin	58
Whisper	58
Dissembling	58
Unstoppable	59
Agelessly	59
Life: the Weather	59
Tonight's Lullaby	60
Always Remember	60
Never Infinite	60
The Moon & Neon Light	60
Imprisoned	61
What else	61
To the People Who Read But Never Comment (On a Poetry Forum)	61
From the Light of Memories	61
For the Sake of Your Life	62
Memoir	62

All About Lies 62
To Rain 62
If You Believe 63
Only When You Light It 63
What's There to Have? 63
Taste of Life..64
21st Century 64
I Wonder..64
Dancing Stars...65
Attire..65
Ocean's Insanity 65
For The Love of Trees 65
Sleep Dares Not 66
Heart's Greeting 66
Nothing to Boast..67
Our Immortal Love 67
The Night Knows 67
Distressed...68
To Feel Them All..68
Young Generation 68
Occupied 68
Burning scars..69
Sprinkled..69
Cannabis 69
We Will Rise 70
For a Brand New Start...70
Invaded 70
Stay Away...71
To Wheedle All Evils Away..71
To the Indolent 72
Cancer..72
War 72
Muse of Glory 73
From a Pensive Mind 73
Hard As Rock...73
Rain Lovers 74

Envious 74
Let me 74
Rage 75
Embrace 75
A Glint of Scars 75
Tranced 76
The Man of Many Lives (A Poem for Tony) 77
From Somewhere 78
Holy Dio: the Diver (A tribute to Ronnie James Dio) ... 79
To MJ (A Tribute to Michael Jackson) 82
A Leader's Path 83

28 Verses Untitled 84
290 Thoughts to Ponder... 88

PREFACE

I believe, poetry is the reflection of my geometrical soul which observes life in various shapes and angles. When I write poems, it strengthens my mind and when it comes to reading poetry, I feel – 'Life is Beautiful'

I have been writing little silly rhymes since my childhood; but from the year 2009 my official poetic journey began through online publication. This is my 5th book consists of free verse, rhyming poems and other thoughts. The monotonous city-life I am living in, makes me take a look at this world in a metaphorically philosophical way. Today's world, day by day, is becoming harder to get by, as if it is made of slabs of concrete cruelty with which we have to build our lives without any choice. The reason why I've titled this book 'Fireclay' is because despite being the most ordinary mud, fireclay is resistant to high heat. And all refractory are constructed from it. Telling you the fact, all high heat resistant firebricks are made of fireclay. It is all around us in the nature, but it can only be discovered and seen, when it is uncovered.

This book can be the most ordinary and simple, but the poems within are based on both simplicity and the complex features of our life and living. The themes of the poems are all around us, all we need to do is to see the truth having highly resistance capacity to this world's darkness. Everything we encounter in life I've tried to capture through my poems – joy, agony, love, grief, deceit, romance, darkness, contentment, passion, dreams, elements of nature, our hope, stormy weather, oceanic pleasure, wildlife, beauty of the sky, death - things that we want and what we don't want- are versified here. So, we never know once this book is uncovered like the simple mud fireclay, it may help people to construct their minds positively to do something useful for the benefit of the world.

May the power within words through a book of verses be our guiding light to life....

Munia Khan
Sunday, October 20, 2019
Dhaka, Bangladesh.

Acknowledgements

I'd like to dedicate this collection of my poetry to all the oppressed people in the world. I will not mention specifically who they are…I will leave it to my readers to comprehend because we all know when we suffer from the oppression of spirit: it could be a war victim, it could be a poverty stricken child or a homeless person or even it could be you and I….

And my special thanks goes to my mentor friend, artist and poetry teacher, Poet RH Peat (Ronald H. Peat) who was born in Sacramento, California and now living at 390 Duncan Hill Road, Auburn, California — 95603. I am eternally in debt to Ron for his kind, unconditional support and encouragement since 2010.

Reflected Stance

I believe the night I've never met
hides one elusive star I need
to divide me between darkness and light

Hope toughens its stance
space: strained
as strange is the way of this world-
if a small ray of light behind the distance
struggles to find me,
miles seem like an illusion

Perhaps the immutable night will soften…
I believe, it will.

Fireclay

This is made of fireclay
Muddy thoughts cannot flay
Those skins from sand and rocks
But it truly unlocks
A simple brick-door: closed
With the truth-key, exposed!

ALONG THE SHORE

It was the seventeenth September of my life
when my heart was floating
on the north side of the Alps; on a lake!
People named it Lake Geneva;
but I called it "Heart Lake"
as it flowed into my heart's core
through the grace of its royal serenity
And in disguise of a fountain
Jet d' Eau was there every second
to pump 500 liters of my excitement
to the height of 140 meters
towards the limitless sky
as if it wanted to be
the symbol of my youthful vigour
instead of symbolizing
Switzerland's strength and vitality
I loved the afternoon sun playing
with its own rays along the shore
And while I was going to meet
the flowers and sculptures of Montreux,
I smelled Lord Byron's ink
sweating an amazing darkness out
from the medieval body of Chillon Castle
Right away I had to stop
Yes, I had to;
not because I read "The Prisoner of Chillon"
but because of a magical effect
the castle's external splendour cast upon me
They said "it was one of the most
feared dungeons in the whole world";
but strangely my mind sensed something else
During those moments, I was happy being imprisoned
by a certain dejection I could never express
I felt I didn't want to leave that place

I began to inhale the breeze
carrying ancient love and mercy
reflected by the lake
The architectural beauty
of the oval-shaped Château de Chillon
buried all its historical mortification and guilt

ALTERED

No one cares about an injured leg of a tiny ant
It has to be healed for its own walking
Such is the norm of nature
which seems to be always unwilling to compromise
How about humanity: human in sanity or human insanity?
Perhaps the definition has altered
Certainly the sun thinks twice nowadays
before rising up to shine on a world
which, in the past, was probably unprepared
to embrace Adam, Eve and Darwin under the same moon
Now the choice is ours-
whether to be a monkey at heart
or to remain an ape of human descent
to let this cruel world go around a bemused Sun

DREAM REVAMPED

I was named after a bird —
a dead pet of my loving, late father
I wished to meet its tiny feathered body
so lifeless in the cage
(but unfortunately, after a few days I was born)
Perhaps a reincarnation I wanted

as I desired to fly in my mind
in quest of my own soul-bird,
all severed, but unlike human
whose every dream
would be the beginning of a new life
with or without a name...
but that remained a pipe dream
Now, in the course of time,
I've become a cold blooded toad —
'Bufo melanostictus'
as the alleged scientific world labeled me
I love to live double lives,
being a nocturnal amphibian.
Hiding myself in a dark lowland area
I love to make friends with
the dirty-pond-inhabitants hydras:
my faithful neighbours!
I'm proud of my pale, yellow-brown colour pattern,
marked boldly with dark, reddish brown streaks and spots —
a constant reminder of
how fortunate I am,
to be able to escape from
the human dominated, so-called 'clean earth'
I've recently buried my avian dreams
in the dingy slum near my abode
Nature, at present,
is a heaven of luxury for me
where I love to make love
to my water-dependent breeding,
allowing the lunar cycle to dictate my ovulation
(Yes, just before or after a full moon occurs)
I dream to lay a long string of black eggs
And I trust, in time my offspring
will begin to reign over humanity
through our sweet sojourn, the vernal pool —
A peaceful place
far away from the man-made world!

Near a Lighthouse

I wish to spend a lifetime
near a lighthouse
where loneliness
will be the glimmer of luminous prancing
upon ocean waves…
rising and falling
only for my breathing…

Deceitful

You can learn things from a heart so bleeding
When love bargains with deceitful pleading
Hours soar from dawn to dawn splitting your time
Don't hear melody from a soundless chime

Hollow Deeds

The center of my sins
stuck behind a blocked door,
circled by hollow deeds
spread on my lifetime's floor

STARS BETWEEN

In a bizarre world behind reality,
two quarrelsome suns
quibble over who's to rise in the east
and who's to set in the west

Days are torn,
and twilight trembles
as nights darken into the depth of dimness
…all asudden, the moon comes out,
in between the suns
to restore peace,
saying –
'Wait till the stars start glittering alive.
They will guide you to your dawn.
They will lead you to a safer dusk.'

The trust in the moon by the suns
dawned their endurance
…and the waiting begins
until reality makes them one
for a brand new universe

SAILING LOVE

Souls of love breathlessly sail
Towards our time when hours fail
To cope with longing here we are
Chasing the speed of a falling star
Miles and miles fleetly we go
Down to the ocean, deeper the flow
Waves now know their crushing tide
Splashing between joy and pride

Eagle's Flight

Eagle's flight of loneliness soars so high
Around its sigh, no more alone the sky
Other birds remain away, clouds pass by
Between shrouds of life and haze sun rays die

Trees

(I)

Let all the green leaves be mine
as long as the trees define
shades created by their limbs
for the soil made with victims
of atrocity's vileness
to redeem the fragileness

(II)

Earth stays in joy
When we plant a tree
Beneath the ground, oh, boy!
Roots feel free

(III)

Nature has no beauty forbidden
Manmade concrete slab: guilt-ridden
Wings or leaves whatever we may care
Those limbs with the birds only trees will share

Riddle's Death

Give me one more night to taste the dark
When wolves imitate a lone dog's bark
Let those secrets remain unspoken
Fallen angel's heart now lover's token
Light grows dim burying riddle's death
Just breathe to free your one last breath

Predicament

There lives a weeper
in each of us-
a silent mourner honoring our despair,
when our willingness slain by helplessness
continues to resurrect to be slaughtered again

After eating three times a day
My sentience wonders - what should I do with the rest of my food?
Aren't these nutrients craved by the starved world around me
engulfed with poverty's hunger?

After sending out two drops of tears, I embrace pause
I still wonder- what am I going to do with the rest of my teardrops?
Aren't those wasted water droplets
soaked by my body's salt contaminated sorrow?

Towards the Waves

Take my hand
and…
feel the sand
beneath your aimless feet
towards the sparkling waves

Never Allow

If it is time you are talking to
Don't forget the path you are walking through
Sudden flare of past might stalk you
Never allow moments to mock you

Being Empty

(I)
What can we expect from an empty shell
Where many hearts of pearl once beat to dwell
Waves fail to break hard layer's bond of love
Wailing shore sends memoir to the sky above

(II)
Being empty makes me whole sometimes
I wonder if every hollow hole
has its own solidity of fulfillment

Mutual Friends

Dawn and dusk are mutual friends of the sun;
one opens the door for him to a brand new day
and the other one has to shut it
to embrace the darkness of night

To Feel A Tranquil Life

Let my toes teach the shore
how to feel a tranquil life
through the wetness of sands

Let my heart latch the door
of blackness, as all my pain
now blue sky understands

City Night

We can't tell if ever night falls asleep
Our slumber veils many secrets: deep
The moonlit visage of this city life
Shines through the blade from a glistening knife
Empty roads now bored of street dogs' barking
Yet nothing tires the underground lurking

Abode

Happiness dwells in every corner of your home
and if you are homeless,
it lives under the leaves of trees,
hiding beneath the sky's cloudiness.
All you need to do is to find it with patience.
Remember, a soul needs something more
than just four walls and a ceiling
It needs permanence through love's shelter,
roofed with affectionate care
like a child's crib lulling reality to dream
until morning tiptoes over for peace

Vincible

All curves and silhouettes
under the state of erratic waning,
and the twilight seems invidious.
It simply can't let the sun hide away
when darkness is just another name for night.

The night where fear consumed
into its deepest shade..
I remember,
the colour of fear is never dark or black;
it is having the colour of thunderbolt;
usually white,
but can appear in different hues
depending on how the fear travels through
to get in your heart.

So, I prefer
to let my heart take it all in;
because nothing is dismayed
in front of a vincible fright

Rejoice

Rejoice with glitters of ashes tonight
Sparkling for moon's spiced silver bite
Upon skin of darkness, loving night more
Storm begins unlocking cold wind's door

Sleepless Soul

My body weeps to live
when you make me believe
that someday I will be dead
Soul sleepless in graveyard's bed

Unharboured

Waves roll in pain, caressed by rain
Kissing shore's lips, lone starfish weeps
Nothing to gain from storm's disdain
Sailed away ships harboured like creeps
Where do you think we'll dive to sink
If not fate saves us from black caves
Life in a blink of an eye's wink
Can leave us now to sate time's vow
All we allow; not knowing how

Shadows of Clouds

All shadows of clouds the sun cannot hide
like the moon cannot stop oceanic tide;
but a hidden star can still be smiling
at night's black spell on darkness, beguiling

STARTLED

Do not trap yourself into an owl's hooting sound
where sad nights linger through the blackness of a hound
Those perplexed angels: still in the conference room
to find out the mystery of the grim bride's groom
Fate knows all secrets behind the wedding planner
when barking and howling groaned in the same manner
Seems life and cruelty are now getting married
to relight this war-world with their burnt flesh: buried!

WHEN YOU FEEL SAD

You don't need a sad soul
to feel the beauty of a dead grave
Just stay with the pale moon
when darkness wants the night to be brave

MY MUSING

I grasp words for the sake of clutching
My mind considers them heart touching
Right then I write for my reader's pleasure
Not knowing what distance a soul can measure

From the Diary of an Old Train

Time won't leave me alone, I know
So, I begin to start
In the name of moments I run
I stop and I run again
I stop; again I run

I'm an old witness
carrying many lives of different hearts everyday
Perhaps that's why my life carries
the burden of an enormous weight and inertia,
therefore, I cannot stop whenever I want
I warn and warn
I warn them through the derailed sound
of my hard breathing
And their misunderstanding calls it the whistle song
But trust me, I never whistle
It is my steamy breath
creating an audible rapture;
sometimes a scream of fright
to a self-sacrificed fool
beneath my heavy existence

Unlike them I move on a fixed track
I love this dependable way
for my wheel shaped legs to walk on;
but I hate my compartmentalized body
as I know no class
No color of skin, no rich, no poor

Upper, middle, lower- engulfed inside my stomach
I digest them all while my rumbling voice
tries to hide the steady chug of my burp

Despite having a disciplined life, I believe,
I'm the only free spirit in the world
who enjoys living free
between the shelter of wind and horizon
where pieces of grassland have their vastness
only to yield to my resolute journey
The lakes and rivers look above
to adore my wingless flying with the birds
when the bridges feel my footsteps
blessing their grateful limbs
Tree trunks: in awe, as branches bow
to inhale the smell of my coal, wood and oil

As I keep on running
the sun goes down kissing me Good Night
with those twilight-lips
And in the dark,
moonlight becomes my night's transport
on which I ride on behind the mountain trails
I sense the seasons smothering me day by day:
sometimes with the purity of a white winter,
often through the damp wetness of raindrops
and sometimes with the fallen leaves of the fall
or with the shiny summer ray of heat

But nothing makes me stationless
as I have to stop
railing my way with a stationary emotion
Yes, I have to stop
to let a little girl step down from me
to visit her father's grave
And I have to welcome on board
the lady in labour pain going to hospital
in quest of her newborn

Life comes and goes
thriving and withering
with me, through me, around me
But will I ever stop running?
Perhaps I won't
Maybe I will…

MISLED

Spring can still be felt
even if you lay under the bed
Frozen heart can melt
in coldness when wintry love misled

LIGHTNING AND RAINBOW

In a world of love
lightning and rainbow
are lovers now
They arc and strike
upon the horizon of credence
to rise above their cloudy vow

PELICAN

Sturdy swimmers afloat on water-couch
Beneath the heavy bill their treasured pouch
Fishes pray for them to fly far away
Inland lakes toast to the Pelican's day

From Another World

One can never imagine
a place like this
where only strange things
are in a state of bliss.

Here, the trees know not
why breeze becomes wind,
Rhinos are lizards,
getting thin skinned!

All frogs are spiders
under umbrella web
And oceans become ponds,
learning to ebb.

Crows and cockroaches
are the best friends here

Together they fly,
leaving pigeons in fear.

Beetles bite the back
of silk moth's pride,
Snails are sitting
on a roller coaster ride.

Rabbits dumping carrots
to feed their pet parrots,
Foxes gift chicken
a pair of boots from Harrods!

Wolf meows in daylight
and cats howl at night,
Caterpillars' racing-car driving
gives the road a fright.

Horses are zebras
with artificial stripes,
Ants eat bitter flowers
of many rare types.

Innocent snakes are
the prey of fireflies,
Flies are accused of
telling all the lies.

Jealous fat rats are
in search of mouse,
Lions mourn for
the tiger's spouse.

After the fish-feast at lunch
cats swim in rivers,
Finding dead deer on board the boat,
fisherman quivers.

The poor starved hyena
looking for some food,
Woodpecker is hooting
as owl pecks the wood.

Police hippo arrests
ugly ducklings, cows, sheep,
Most herons are busy
digging mole holes, deep.

Eagles shave their necks
pretending to be vultures,
Cocoons are adapting
different cultures.

Birds imitate
butterflies and moths,
Lambs are in need of
woollen cloths.

Lice live in bald head,
mosquitoes drink milk in bed,
To let human suck blood
out of human instead.

All the dogs now are apes
hiding their tails,
Monkeys become donkeys
when banana-peeling fails.

Only clowns are allowed
to wear the crowns,
The white, black, green, grey-
all here are browns,

From the smuggler's smiling teeth
gold is found,
Poppies are roses
spread on drug lover's ground.

The sun knows no future,
only sky can tell
When will the earth
really start to swell.

In anguish and grief
it'll shake and quake,
The lake will forsake
all swans that are fake.

Rain drains the cloud
to get smoke out of fume,
All perfumes of the world
the dumpsters consume.

This is the world
inside a corrupted world,
where crystalline green glass
is called emerald.

A rebirth we need
for a peaceful place
to save humanity
from fatal disgrace

TO ZAIMA: MY DAUGHTER

I'm two days away
from day after tomorrow
Counting the hours
to my upcoming sorrow
Suddenly I look
into the eyes of my child
Then all sadness gone
as I smile the way she smiled

New Year's Eve

Many yesterdays will stream together
on this Thursday night;
not to lament the past
but to jubilate
another egocentric excursion
of earth around the sun.
I still don't know how to react
to this renewed vanity of nature
Perhaps, I'll be amused
by the sun's pretense
to be a light from the sky-candle
...after all, it's time's birthday!
Even the grass-blades
would love to cut the cake of moments.

Taste of Your Words

(A poem with 4-5-4-5 syllable counts)

Still in my mouth
the taste of your words
Wind from the south
now inhaled by birds

Gently you speak
like murmured river
Sunrays to stick
to trees which quiver

For your great heart
The woods gets deeper

Fairies depart
You're the moon keeper!

In the forest
Under the blue sky
Together we rest
As in love we fly

EMPTY WINDS

Storm gathers empty winds reliant on thunder
If horizontal rain falls straight down- I wonder
Neutral sky expands the gloom; every bolt is cursed
Strong hail starts to drip as hunger becomes a thirst

HOLD MY HAND

Let our love chase all clouds away
Hold my hand and feel the day
Your footsteps guide my steps all along
Beneath my skin your veins belong

CANDLELIT LOVE

There's a silent movement of heart
Gently beating to feel you
Our love-struck days: on the alert
When souls burn in reddened hue

Our divine passion sips desire

Like moonbeams absorb the night
Your boundless love takes me higher
Through a timeless dreamy flight

You're always near to let me hear
Every whisper from your lips
Your unseen gaze to me so dear
Your bare thoughts my mind worships

There's nowhere to flee or to hide
I'll dwell in your loving arms
The Rule of love I've to abide
Until, for us, dream alarms

Feel the strength of your weakened knees
Through this bond of friendship tight
Always here the heavenly breeze
relighting love's candle light

When You Are Gone

May be you are gone,
but that doesn't make me come back
Night never meet the dawn
yet nothing makes it fear the black

Armored

The sky can never be frozen
because its vastness has chosen
all warmth of our lives as we look above
with unbreakable hearts armored in love

Palestine

Blood is everywhere..
Vultures take shelter beneath the tanks;
for the fumed sky is unsafe for their avian flight
to prey on the Palestinian flesh

Atonement

(I)

(A mono rhyme with 9 syllables per line)
Every known thing used to be unknown
And every rock could become a stone
Someday nature will have to atone
When soul sees dead flesh leaving the bone

(II)
...and when we die
we die alone
I cry, I cry alone
Like a piece of stone
I am thrown
into the wavy ocean of life
to atone...to atone
Only to atone...

Mingling With the Green

I've learnt to gather simplicity from grasshoppers.
I like their naive indecisive minds
never knowing exactly when to stop chirping,
and I envy their ability
to be able to mingle with the green…

Poor Dear Piano

There was no music theory
of the minor fall or the major lift
It was a vagary from my dreamy state
where my sleepy brain-cells drift
with no cartoon gag of El Coyote
trying to catch the Road Runner
but with a piano falling
upon a Saturday night stunner
For me it was a dream, no nightmare
as it was a musical piano, not a flying dead crow
It was not falling from the sky
but from a rooftop which allowed to grow
a garden of liars having hydrological benefits
The piano was the eye-witness
of their secret meetings with the so-called Lithophytes
It wondered about those lying plants' unfitness
Sitting into the flowerpots of power,
they planned to control the city temperature
through their disguised greenness
They were something else, not the plants: miniature!
The piano knew it; So, it decided to jump
from that high raised building's top
right on the head of one of those herbs
who pretended to be a Saturday night beauty
And the TV reporters used no pronoun, just nouns and verbs…
Only to hide and be secretive about the gender
And at heart everybody felt so tender
They reported- "The piano fell on someone walking down the road.
The person had minor injuries and was taken to a safe abode"
And then the destroyed parts of the piano they showed.
Only the piano knew that the mysterious person
upon whose head it fell was a politician
Suddenly I woke up from my dream and realized-
For the poor piano, there was no funeral, no mortician
Because it was an inanimate object
But it was the only one knowing the truth…
Yes, the only one..

Wilted And Empty

Sometimes it is easier
to feel the veins wilted and empty
than to sense the coldness of blood in fear

Remembrance

We'll know where to find the fleeting time
When our childhood smiles through a nursery rhyme
We'll know how to grasp our days gone by
When the gifts from our lost-ones we hold and sigh
Let us not talk about memories
Let us cherish them instead
Our restless heart might feel at ease
Treasuring the past from the dead

Raindrop

When you become a raindrop in your mind
Thunder is the closest friend you may find
Wind lashed trees, dark clouds, lightning or the dust
Everything you will bear once you adjust

We Can Never Tell

Mountain may want to be with the stream
To climb the hills perhaps a river's dream
What we want exactly we may never know
Flame of fire might love to melt with the snow

Maybe the bee wants the eagle's wingspan
Neighbour may desires to be a kinsman
Banana may want to be squeezed like a lime
A foe might wish to be a partner in crime

Crimson sky might want more of blood red
Maybe the chair wishes to sit on a bed
Spinning is perhaps what the blades of fan dread
The poor may want only a piece of bread

From bitter truth the lies wishes to escape
Circle of love wants to live in heart's shape
Silhouette of dying trees twilight engraving
As we keep on spending life, longing and craving!

Into the Bonfire

Where ever we go, whatever we earn
the time we waste can never return
The mistakes we've made are now to burn
into the bonfire of guilt and wrongdoing
Will we ever learn to stop pursuing
those temptations of life that minds are wooing?

Electronic

Life is full of electronic desires
where one dream spliced with currents of wires
Leading our footsteps to the online shore
we expect the waves to bring us some more
of those binary tides to wash us away
to the cyber beach for a lonesome day

Never an Unborn

Here I am, after the conception process,
savouring my embryonic self,
constantly growing-
the size of a kidney bean.
I have become host
to a quickly beating heart and now,
learning to love the way how
my intestines are forming these days.
Sensing how my eyelids, mouth, nose, earlobes,
are taking shape gradually; I am alive!
Perhaps this is the life-miracle,
of which I am still not aware.
I don't know what to do with this newly formed
skin, hair, lenses of eyes,
tooth enamel and the nervous system.
Not sure what life really is,
but I can imagine,
since my tiny, unique finger prints
are in place already: quite evidently
Yes, life is here while I'm still a fetus
Yet, I hate this growth spurt,
where I am about the size of a tasteless avocado;
Nevertheless, I'm delighted,

for my heart is now pumping more blood each day.
As the weeks go by,
I wonder at my skeleton hardening
from rubbery cartilage to bone.
(Maybe it's for the best of my staying alive strongly)
I love to share the joy
of developing: my ability to hear,
so I let my mother feel those little flutters and kicks!
I'm really overwhelmed with my brain impulses;
I feel totally blessed by this prenatal development
My arms, hands, legs, feet- progressing faster.
Fully formed brain, newly formed nails,
my developed face, nerve cells connection to the brain
everything secures my entity
I am growing
Yes, I am growing!
I'm stretching out
from head to bottom.
I can squint and frown
with more powerful kicks and prods;
am not going to drown
into the pool of joy;
am whirling like a toy
from north to south;
Wow! Now I can open my mouth
Am saving my weight and length
Stronger I feel with all my strength!
Every part of me becomes more distinct
Am looking more like a human
I can grasp tight now, you know.
I feel I'm going to clutch the entire world,
because now I know I'm a girl
My lungs love to breathe through another existence.
My wrinkled skin begins to smooth out
I feel light filters in through the womb
I just can't wait to see the light of another world

Not sure how it will be
Will it be a world full of peaceful fluids,
where I can float and swim?
Or it will be a damp place,
just to grow up and survive?
...I wonder
I really wonder...
People call me the 'unborn',
but I am not;
as I call myself a 'child'
born months ago
in the safest place on earth:
my mother's womb!

Create Your World

Heaven dwells
in the murmuring sound
of a beautiful river
Hell burns beneath the ocean
on the horizon of which
sun loathes to sink every day
Where on earth do you believe
the world lives..?
Inside your heart for sure
And it spins around your sadness
where you can create your own moon
to smile upon your life...

Summer 2018

Summer, this year, is full of rain
As if heat mourns with the world of pain
Is it an aching smile or a joyful cry?
The sky knows it best, but we must try
To rise with the sun, not to set with him
By being a star when the twilight's dim

Mortality's Song

Ashes have no fear to burn in hell
In your heart's paradise angels dwell
Rib cage fastens all sins of the wrong
Your bones will sing you mortality's song

Peacefully Tanned

When the tidal waves wildly behaving
My bare feet on the shore busy saving
The calm warmth leaking out of the sand
To let my heart feel peacefully tanned!

APART

You let go of my hand
to hold on to my heart
Distance grasps us tight;
now that we are apart

I will keep on loving you until
eternity comes to make me love you more

IF I WERE

If I were a flower,
humming bird would be my favourite bee
And If I were blind,
the light of darkness I'd love to see

Adieu to My Twisted Being

(Steve Jobs from his Death Bed)

Just a single bite from an Apple
And my heart was doomed
Never desired to be
the Adam of the technological heaven
because ironically to be capitalized
there 'I' had to be a small 'i'

Now breathing hard,
I feel this bed of death, eventually,
has made a transaction with my real wealth:
the goldmine of unconditional love
from my treasured flesh and blood- my family!

Today, mortality has introduced poverty
to my soon-to-be-fled soul
Remorse: my only currency!
And success…?
Well, none of my business anymore
as the burden of my expansive career
filled with expensive jobs
I'm leaving behind with my last name

How You Love Me

How you love me I can tell
Words of bewitching magic spell
Ring for the love, ring the bell
Restrain emotions; organ to swell
Together "you and I" forever dwell
Under the sky or in a prison cell
We can make heaven to hate the hell
No buying of soul, no dreams to sell
Because how you love me I can tell.

Truth

Truth will keep on telling the truth
Lies will lie to be more uncouth
No more rainbow after the storm
Nowhere to escape leaving the norm

From the Passionate Vine

I tell you this before it starts to rain
What you have done, please do it again
Despite of the thorns, we pluck the rose
Feel my impatience for I need you close
My heart is aroused by your secret sign
Let me feel your bones and your bold spine
Imbrue me with your reflected figure
I embrace your vigour for I'm so eager
The passion of your mind so well set
A lover like thee in my dreams I've met
I'll keep on loving, you be careful or not
Upon the silk sheet will you pierce the spot?
My hands reach out to touch your face
As your lips are touching the curves of grace
Beyond the desire my veins start searching
Our blood so hot- moves in order for marching
On my mouth your warm breath I start tasting
Your lips on mine so sensationally pasting
In quest of heaven the electric eel
Smoldering, melting into the love we feel
In ecstasy ourselves we keep sating
Missing heartbeats, faster pulsating
Everywhere we love, leaving world behind
Our pure pleasure soulfully we bind
Skin to skin, heart to heart as one we recline
Flesh goes on pleasuring as you are mine
The stream of our love will never run dry
Nectars mingle with the joyful cry
You pour me all your love; drop by drop
Expect me not my love to tell you to stop
I tell you this before it starts to rain
Love is the game where we both will gain
Gain the paradise out of this Earth
As our souls talk and achieve the mirth
We taste the wine from our passionate vine
Stay forever as our moons to align

EVERYTHING YOU ARE

You're my moonlit love of caressed night
My soulful star twinkling for me right
My feathered pillow's soft touch you are
On secret place my gripped clutch you are
You are my flame for I'm your Eve
You're my Adam who'll never deceive
You're the thrust of my deepest core
My only entrance to my long closed door
You're my motion for riding hard
You're the love-milk within my dripping curd
You're my paradise to heavenly height
My loving licks to taste and bite
My kissing joy of love you are
Into my heart a white dove you are
You're my days with all my longing
The sole owner of my heart's belonging
Between my thighs the fingertips you are
Joyride of my bouncing hips you are
You're the pulse of my core's squeezing
My strong caress for your heart's pleasing
You're the tight suction of my walls
My heavenly helmet and delicious balls
Everything you are, as you are my life
To slay my hunger, my amorous knife
You're my angel owning my wings
You're all the cords of my heart's strings

To the Wise Cupid

How can I be the mentor of a Cupid?
In front of your sensuous words mine are stupid
How come a master like you be teachable?
When your mind is everywhere reachable
Everywhere around through my desirous vein
Yes, you are all over; for I am slain
By the God of romance with his sword of passion
When on the moon wet-night has no aggression
But tonight you will be my pupil of love
I'll be your teacher from the school of heart above
I'll teach you how purely to discover me
By closing your eyes my heart you'll see
I'll teach you where or how to love more
The discovered land through a forbidden door
Your breath will learn from my lip's touch
How to inhale me deep with warm love much
And my breath will teach you how to be fragrant
Being my student, this love should you grant?
My breasts will teach you to be a starving child
My tongue's touch on your ears will teach you to be wild
My arousal will show you how to have erection
While spread legs give points to passion's resurrection
Your nose will be my favourite student
And my suction will teach you how to be prudent
Your shoulder will learn from my hand's caress
Your skin will be reading my fingertips' press
My scared place will teach how to drip good
Your helmet will learn from my wall's wet mood
Your touch will take a lesson from my winged heat
Which answers all questions on the G spot's beat
You will learn to write on my womanhood's sheet
Between the chapters of my thighs your pen will fit
From my lips your manhood will learn to swell
Inside my moist path your hardness will dwell

From behind me into my core your thrust: ardent
Will learn how to hit from my posture so bent
Towards paradise you will learn to ride
I'll teach your back how to lay on your side
Then your bums will be taught how to be sucked
My feast on your balls will teach you to be f**ked
From my mouth your mouth will learn to drink
I'll teach your hardened rod how to shrink
Your body will learn from my faster motion
When I'll teach you to pour hot milky potion
You'll learn from my curves how not to be coy
Then my warmth will take you to a class of joy
There you'll score high with your ravishing spine
When we'll be as one and I'll make you mine......

DECEIVER

Here's something about a liar I know:
he can wake you up when you're wide awake.
And when you're asleep
nightmares foisted upon your dreams
by his mendacity
want you to become an insomniac.
He is filthy powerful,
as he can make you spit on your own credulity.
Every time you fall for his falsehood,
your trapped gaze of innocence
feels cramped to stare at his blue-eyed assurance.
He pretends to be colour-blind
and repels to believe -
A lie has many colours,
while white is the only faithful colour of truth.
He will introduce you to some tangled heartstrings,
if you ever realize that your eyes need to be opened

wider than your heart,
when love is blinder than your eyes.
Is it a fiction when in the name of his blood
he swears- "I'm not a liar" ?

TINY ABODE

Sitting in a corner, I live like a toad
Oh! How I love my room: my tiny abode!
Here I wake up; and I sleep in here
The world far away; yet virtually near
Not that I'm jailed in this place of grace
Just don't want to face another face

TO THE QUEEN OF TREES (PART I)

A Tribute poem to Sycamore Fig Tree

She still remains the tree: sycamore fig
Blue sky grins upon her motherly limbs
Beetle's love bites on her green veins to dig
Deeper holes of life until sunlight dims
She feeds wild lives through her body n' shades
Weaker chicks of hornbills, red ants, bees, wasps
Hilda bugs nymphs breathe till existence fades
Her greenness survives when parasite clasps
Their hatching and breeding brings back lost hope
As life drowned in dew drops buried 'neath her
With spider's crawl, grim snakes she learns to cope
Her fruit: crocodile's bait; monkey leaves scar
Black human, green pigeon or pink mantis
Great years they live to be her apprentice

TO THE QUEEN OF TREES (PART – II)

A Tribute poem to Sycamore Fig Tree

Between the sun and clouds fig tree grows old
Rain awakes her lethargic companion
Cicadas-assault-squirt she learns to hold
She's proud being sycamore, never banyan
Her fruit drips to sate vinegar fly's thirst
Her open arms branches: avian home
Torn fresh leaves: killer predator's outburst
Wild lives become stained glass of her life's dome
Guest elephants from far she likes to serve
Her trunk and their trunks as if connected
Ignoring guard ants, reptiles have the nerve
To eat her sugary bliss: collected!
She's the heaven for all mammals- bats, deer
For Africa she'll stay still always here

JUST TO SWING

Her mother's prudence is not going to be her guide
She thinks- "That's not me! I'm never gonna swallow my pride"
She loves to sway on that rope swing hanging
her longing from the youth-tree
pushing herself back and forth over the
shallow pond of generation gap
How many times she preaches back her mom - she really cannot tell!
Faith is just a belief which remains alive between heaven and hell
Being a Muslim, her mom wants her to cover her head
She wonders what if she wears a bikini and then covers her head!
Perhaps with a Hijab or maybe with a swim
cap which her mom will dread

Will it make her any purer than she already is?
Will that make her parents happy?
She feels devilish realizing she must be
possessed by that Goosebumps' Slappy
No! No wicked mask of evil spirit belongs to her innocent being
It is that wild fragrance from the essence of
freedom which she wears to swing

Through the Verse of Blood

His tearful verse bleeds
Pain soundlessly leads
the way to a lonely river
where rippled water flows to shiver
for his solitary vanity
untamed by memory's insanity
He will write on dripping the blood
Nature will treasure that soul-felt flood

Afterlife

Think how we'll let the ground
to hold our weight
How time is not around
to fall for the bait
of this life so trapped
and awfully fleeting
Think how souls:unwrapped
will meet the greeting

Listen Hard

If you are the voice,
I am your whisper
Stronger than a loud noise
Spread from mouth to ears
Treasuring the sound for million years

Shark

Into the sea I'd love to sink
When with both eyes a shark can blink
Is he a brave fish or a marine man?
Through those closed eyelids my heart will he scan?

A Pair of Love Poems

(I)
You are the star of my moonless night
In the darkness my dazzling light
I heal my soul loving you more
In search of you- night sky I explore
Beneath the clouds there you are
Twinkling away my true love from afar

(II)
In the days of winter, you are my spring
In my blue heart all the red joy you bring
You are my mountain of hope and desire
Conquering the hills of sadness on fire
In the middle of dark sky you're my star
My loving Angel from heaven you are

Our love will shine like the sun of dawn
I'll breathe for you till my life is gone

Rhyme From an Insomniac

When pain is so hurtful
we want it to be dead;
but throwing stones of heartache
we keep it alive instead
Then sometimes my heart
is equal to sadness
Should the balance of my life
demand madness... ?
'Cause crazy things around
messing up my head.
Where is the bed of roses?
Are these roses for bed?
Million more questions
all night and day
making me sleepless enough
to feel my hair turned grey

In Love with Memories

As I woke up in my morning bed
My love soaked heart no more misled
Your memories just held me tight
After a long dismal lonely night
Our soaring souls knew how to love
Each part of our bodies: beneath, above
Being in passion left us breathless
My love for you: forever deathless!

The Dying One

(This is a poem written in collaboration with the very talented poet Doug Sandvick better known as Simon Johann Andresen, author of the book "Fannie : Poems Inspired by Frances Fannie Benjamin Johnston". The first three stanzas written by Doug. And last two stanzas written by me)

Is this death
or a form of slumber?
Someone bend a branch.
I pray it does not snap.

In the harshness of winter,
I despise the other trees.
They sway as one in the wind,
a plurality of shelter.

My height was never a degree
to judge myself with others.
I was always stunted
but born a little older.

Now my aging stands firm
all exposed and bare
derided by their veiled greenness
to hide the crude sweeping

Beneath my roots
I have planted life
for the dead and mortals
And the waning of self is so alive!

On Your Birthday

On a day like today
the sun shines upon the flower's smile,
warming the softness of petals
And into the woods a vibrant pixy dances
along with her fairytale joy
to wish you a Happy Birthday

On a day like today
river whispers to the gentle breeze
begging it to dream for a while
And trees surrender to all singing birds
to wish you a Happy Birthday

On a day like today
hours wait for the night to caress all stars,
bathing into their twinkling love
And the moon melts in pleasure of living
to wish you a Happy Birthday

On a day like today
simplicity breaks the rule of wildness
in a lonely state of ecstasy
And fire burns to sate the fading candle
to wish you a happy birthday

Word-Power

Being stuck in my room,
I've become a world traveler.
If you wonder how...
just guess how I've reached you right now

Under My Skin

I climb the door instead of a tree
Just to crawl with myself walking free
What if I'm a lizard beneath my skin
Changing my colors of the human I've been

Whisper

There is a whisper of light
if you can hear
Louder than sound of darkness
you never fear
Numb sky's muteness
leaves you hard of hearing
Senses wish to fly;
feelings disappearing

Dissembling

Wind and breeze are separated today
Crimson twilight denies to fade away
Grass blades turn brown to match the soil
We pretend to smile at every turmoil

Unstoppable

She was the creator of her own fate
There was no sun, since she woke up late
Only night was around with greetings, dark
Wrong choices she made still there to lurk
The path she chose was not steppable
Her stumblings that's why: unstoppable!

Agelessly

When I find myself growing older
Blood in my veins loathes to feel colder
Skin: in pain giving birth to wrinkles
Still with the stars my soul's light twinkles

Life: the Weather

Hurricane chases us
but we chase life
So, life is not a hurricane
Life is the weather itself
We hardly can control it
It controls us
Sunny life, stormy life, cloudy life, rainy life
All control us
And somewhere beneath those dark clouds peace hides.
Sometimes our rainy hearts wash it away
Sometimes the sun within us makes it come alive

Tonight's Lullaby

Sleep like you can never be dead
Dream as if you have a soul inside your head
Go to bed; go to bed
Catch a moon so red
Or purple instead

Always Remember

Faded wound may knock you back
To remind you of the past things it'll attack
So, always remember how you're maimed
Before you find that your future is aimed!

Never Infinite

Crossing the limit is not my style
My footsteps meander less than a mile
I travel the world perhaps in a minute
Yet a dream, to me, is never infinite!

The Moon & Neon Light

Moon is a superstar to a neon light
Both are in doubt of their lifeless plight
One envies the sun, the other one's scared
But to face the dark they're always prepared

Imprisoned

When we do not know our heart's reason
Perhaps living inside the cell of its prison
Is the best way to breathe for the life of love
With pain of the void from a distance above

What else

What else there can be between shadows and mirages
If not my diffused self struggles to hide my deserted life
What else there will be between time and ages
If not my tender hope remains to surmount all strife

To the People Who Read But Never Comment (On a Poetry Forum)

Some people decide not to comment at all
Perhaps they read it, or do they read that all?
Still we'll taste them; we'll pour some sugar of likes
We never tumble; our poetry-shoes have some spikes

From the Light of Memories

Life becomes meaningful with a loving heart's gift
Upon the ocean of gratitude soul's boat adrift
Invisible expectancy tossed and turned
From the light of memories a blessed ray earned

For the Sake of Your Life

Every time I try to be your veins
to take love-blood toward your heart,
you act like arteries: always busy carrying it away from the <u>heart</u>;
yet I'm glad your act is vital for sustaining life

Memoir

I gave you my heart.
You gave it back to me- all bruised, and lifeless.
But I will keep on living
so that I could save this heart
as a memoir of all our loving

All About Lies

When he lied
Wish my hands were tied
Behind his heart
Clutching its beating filled with dirt
When he lied

To Rain

Rain,
Aren't you my soul's joyful tears
only longing for the sky to be happy?

If You Believe

Smile is the arch of an arrowed heart
Tears are waters to make pain's life start
Cry to laugh, take the grief to leave it
Choose what you want, if you believe it

Only When You Light It

A lantern can give you light
only when you light it
When dark clouds give us a fright
sky turns blue to fight it

What's There to Have?

What's there to find in a broken heart
if not assembled pieces of love for a pristine start
What's there to see behind the curtain
only things that you don't know for certain
What's there to lead to a forbidden path
If we keep ignoring sin's aftermath
There's not much to have, yet more to lose
Cloudy sky waits for the lighter shade of blues

TASTE OF LIFE

(I)

When someone breaks your heart into pieces
Don't let it split you up; noting decreases
Your shredded mind will handle it all
Please don't let yourself fall to crawl.
Hang in there, just stand up tight
Such is the taste of life from a single bite

(II)

When sighs are hypnotized by sorrow
Happy moments you need to borrow
From a little child or from a bird
Who has the wild freedom of soul: stirred!

21ST CENTURY

Sitting makes us think of standing
Our current stance keeps on demanding
We wish to fly without the wings
Puppets move before pulling the strings

I WONDER

I've seen that and I ponder
It's not right and I wonder
How we can live to live more
If dark slips through light's door?

Dancing Stars

Stars are always dancing.
Sometimes they dance twinkling away
with the rhythm of your joyful heart;
and sometimes they dance without movement
to embrace your heartache
as if frozen sculptures of open-armed sadness

Attire

Far away soul in a dreamy state
Forgotten slumber seemingly late
Pure rhythmic love now rising higher
Unclad passion our only attire

Ocean's Insanity

If lighthouse becomes a burning candle,
flickered upon ocean's insanity.
Your sailing heart there anchors to handle
the obsessed breeze towards sand dune's vanity

For The Love of Trees

If you can feel the love from a tree,
the life of your heart will surely agree
that its branches, roots and leaves
are connected to your soul as long as it lives

Sleep Dares Not

My heart can feel the softness of a star
Only when the moon stays afar
I lay my mind on the pillow of sky
Where sleep dares not ever to pry

Heart's Greeting

(A Poem with 3 syllables per line)

Our Hearts greet
when souls treat
Love with care
So, we dare
to love more
and adore
each other
like mother
loves her child-
gently mild
pure ever
fake never
Strength in mind
now we find
in our bond
miles beyond...

Nothing to Boast

When you start dreaming- what's there to boast?
Life may treat you like a living ghost
Brokenness haunts you until you perish
Death will bring you nothing to cherish

Our Immortal Love

(I)
Oceanic farness treasures tomorrow
Our mingled tears lost in the sea of sorrow
This immortal love will lead us a way
When pale days remain cloudy and gray
(II)
Your love: like water in a desert land
My heart is into the palm of your hand
In your sacred passion my body thrives
Let's live to love till eternity arrives

The Night Knows

Dark night knows what full moon requires
When all your love my heart acquires
Celestial bodies no more faded
Life makes sound; silence invaded

Distressed

Sorry for being stuck in the traffic
of my mind's stressful road
The world seems very pornographic
I can't carry the load

To Feel Them All

You don't need to be the tide to rise and fall,
you don't have to be a wave to touch the shore;
just be a little sand-grain and feel them all

Young Generation

We're thirsty each moment
Tiny drops of life we sip
When time fails to feed us
Modernity gulps us deep
Now in search of bestowment
Through cyber space we creep

Occupied

Dance away with the song of life
The tune within might erase your strife
Playing with time is not that easy
Yet hope keeps us forever busy

Burning scars

We can imagine some stars,
if there aren't any
We should look after those scars,
fatally burnt many

Sprinkled

There's nothing wrong in dreaming
when you are awake
Reality is brimming
with hunger, love and ache
The sky is unsure
why the arid moor feels bleak
Quaking of earth to lure
the narrowness of creek
Thunder speaks louder
hiding echo from all screams
Dust of starry powder
to sprinkle upon your dreams
There's nothing wrong in hoping
when your wishes are gone
Time's now eloping
with stolen days of dawn

Cannabis

Is there a light behind the sun...?
with which we can have some fun
as our days under the dark still without hope;
yet we taste the trees, they are the dope!

WE WILL RISE

Our breath is to live
Our life is to breathe
Why can't we believe
That we'll rise from under
the ashes of doubt
when all lights are out

FOR A BRAND NEW START

Sea of hurt washes my heart
With waves after waves
But I'll have a brand new start
To be the bravest of the braves

INVADED

Dark night knows what full moon requires
When all your love my heart acquires
Celestial bodies no more faded
Life makes sound; silence invaded

Stay Away

Faded dawn
When I'm gone
Find the sun
Make things done
Who denies
All those lies?
Live alone
Be like stone
Find the day
Stay away

To Wheedle All Evils Away

Upon limbs of life we never need to chew
as Jeffrey Dahmer left us a clue
If there's no racism in eating a nigger
then why did it make him his own grave digger
Sledgehammer, saws or pulling the trigger
can only make monsters; nothing much bigger
We need no knives, no drill-bits, no needle
to bore holes in our conscience to wheedle
all evils away by being luminous and pure
where blackness of the dark finds nothing to lure

To the Indolent

Morning birds are never lazy
But their chirping may drive them crazy
Whoever burns the midnight oil
Not caring if their days to spoil
They sleep all day escaping from light
Midnight wakes them up all so bright
They're not vampires, they're the indolent
Just be curious about them, don't be insolent

Cancer

Cancer is never a lethal disease
If your strength of mind wants it to freeze
Death will arrive, but it loves to wait
When living in hope is never too late

War

One sin leads to another
Brother kills brother
When time: all spare
Who wants to bear
The burden of war
Cowards what we are

Muse of Glory

Starlight beats when heart twinkles
Youthful sky beyond cloudy wrinkles
Muse of glory to flame the night
Verse inscribed as written light

From a Pensive Mind

(I)
Loneliness is not the enemy of your joy
as long as you know how you should always destroy
the pensive mood that remains with you like a friend
who never stands up for you when you're forced to bend

(II)
If I die today, will you remember me tomorrow?
The love I'm leaving behind, will you care to borrow?
From a snake-shed-skin or from the sky unknown
In all living and the dead I'll dwell to groan

Hard As Rock

Sealing your lips makes your eyes talk
Truth creeps beneath your lame feet's walk
Knees stiffen when blood vessels stalk
Lies of pounding heart - hard as rock

Rain Lovers

The moon seems unaware
of night's dark hitting
on the damp warm rain
misguiding owl's spitting
A thunder light of love
raising hearts beating
while weather learns more
from rain lovers meeting

Envious

(A Poem with 5-6-5-6 syllable counts)
Wings can only fly
as long as the bird flies
Soul blackens when you
put on vestment of lies
White candle wax cries
for ignitable wick
Jealous people burn
to make your heart feel sick

Let Me

Let me smell your love like I smell the roses in my garden
Let me touch your heart like I touch the
moonbeams from our night
Let me hold your hand like I hold my breath to inhale you
Let me love you like I love our love

Rage

If you venture to be a sage
Let your virtues subside your rage
For deep wisdom you'll be venerated
Let cold veins feel blood cells generated

Embrace

When twilight sleeps holding the night
In your arms you embrace me tight
Runaway hours clenched by kisses
More of your love my heart misses

A Glint of Scars

Night never needs a shade
but it requires to fade
into the grin of twinkling stars
where light is just a glint of scars

TRANCED

(A Tribute poem to Armin van Buuren celebrating 900th Episode of A State of Trance. Titles of Armin's studio albums are written in uppercase and also titles of Armin's hit songs are included in this poem)

Let us dance
with the State of Trance
May Glory be thine
Armin divine!
Your music flows through rivers
So 'INTENSE', sending 'SHIVERS'
up the spine of the world
As if soul-drops pearled
on rain-soaked windowpanes
Your tunes: blood for our veins
The pure 'MIRAGE' we 'EMBRACE'
is the vision of your grace
Born in Nineteen '76'
You're the lord of Remix
All our 'Blue Fear' you cure
with 'A STATE OF TRANCE' so pure
When we're 'In & Out of Love'
You lift us higher from above
For our 'Beautiful life' the 'Great Spirit' you are!
Guiding us to 'Be In The Moment', you lead us so far
'The Light Between Us' is now 'Heading Up High'
Through your 'Wild Wild Son', who will never die
We're never "Fine Without You", we're 'United'
The blaze of your tune keeps us ignited
In those 'Sunny Days', we're 'Waiting For the Night'
'Another You' gives us the 'Therapy' just right
With your 'Sex, Love & Water' we're 'Burned With Desire'
'This Is A Test' of great 'Ping Pong' only to get higher
We 'Live For That Energy'; no 'Sound of Goodbye'

Even your 'Blah Blah Blah' can make us fly
We're 'Not Giving Up On Love' as long as you're here
'Our Origin' is the 'Orbion' with 'Youtopia' of the year
'This Is What It Feels Like' when we're 'Ready To Rave'
We need to listen to you from the cradle to the grave
You are the DJ Sublime!
Now for the 900th time
You prove it again
Between now and then
We can 'IMAGINE' only you
creating melody anew!

THE MAN OF MANY LIVES
(A POEM FOR TONY)

This poem is written in tribute to my dear friend, the artist, author, public speaker, researcher from British Columbia, Tony Mayo, Author of Twenty-Nine Lives

He creates life with his painting brush
Like crashing waves form the tidal crush
Across the oceans; beneath the sky
His adventures: reborn, never to die
Flying with colours birds' feathers rejoice
Great easel stands by his artistic voice
The avian beaks become ardent lips
Through those sculptured souls from his fingertips
Glasses, ceramics, papers and sands
Breathe to live between his artful hands
His written words can reach the stars: bright
He's the man of many lives vanquishing fright

From Somewhere

(A Tribute poem to my favorite Irish Singer and Song Writer Sarah Lynn using some of her hit song titles)

'Will You Be There Somewhere'
when the 'Ashes' survive
between pain's 'Silhouette' and shadow
as she sings to the 'Sparks After the Sunset'?

Will you 'Look Above' to the 'Gold In the Sky'
when 'A Desert Rose' watches
the 'Water Runs Dry' as she sings
to sprinkle our desolate hearts?

Will you extract 'The Very Center of Me'
to 'Show Me the Stars' when my soul
becomes a 'Dream Weaver' as she sings
to melt the cold moon we share?

'In Winter' she could 'Put You Together Again'
When you 'Dive' with 'Folded Wings'
to find our 'Broken Child' for the 'New Dawn'

'At the End of Every Journey' when 'Hearts Unite'
and 'Love Is Wide Awake'
'You Move Me' with the 'Color of Your Heart'
And I 'Beat Alive' to 'Save Your Last Breath'
for her songs as she sings
for us to breathe

Holy Dio: the Diver (A tribute to Ronnie James Dio)

(A tribute poem to my favorite rock star Ronnie James Dio: Former lead vocalist of the band Rainbow, Black Sabbath. This is written with all the titles of the hit songs of DIO. The titles are all in upper case)

You can "CATCH THE RAINBOW" –
"A RAINBOW IN THE DARK"
Through "ROCK & ROLL CHILDREN"
"HOLY DIVER" will lurk
"BEFORE THE FALL" of "ELECTRA"
"ALL THE FOOLS SAILED AWAY"
"JESUS,MARY AND THE HOLY GHOST"-
"LORD OF THE LAST DAY"

"MASTER OF THE MOON" you are
When my "ONE FOOT IN THE GRAVE"
With our "BLACK", "COLD FEET",
"MYSTERY" of "PAIN" you crave

You're "CAUGHT IN THE MIDDLE",
"BETWEEN TWO HEARTS"
When "HUNGRY FOR HEAVEN"
"HUNTER OF THE HEART" hurts

"FALLEN ANGELS" "FEED MY HEART"
"FEVER DREAMS" "FEED MY HEAD"
"I AM" "ANOTHER LIE"
"AFTER ALL (THE DEAD)"

Not "GUILTY" if you "HIDE IN THE RAINBOW"
With your perfect "GUITAR SOLO"
"DON'T TELL THE KIDS" to "DREAM EVIL"
Don't "GIVE HER THE GUN" to follow

"DON'T TALK TO STRANGERS"
Those "EVIL EYES" can see
"LORD OF THE NIGHT" "MISTREATED";
"MY EYES" hate to fancy

"SHAME ON THE NIGHT" "TURN UP THE NIGHT"
Now it's "TIME TO BURN"
"TWISTED" "VOODOO" does "WALK ON WATER"
And today its our turn

"BLOOD FROM A STONE" "BORN ON THE SUN"
I'm "BETTER IN THE DARK" "BREATHLESS"
The "PRISONER OF PARADISE" you are!
Forever you are deathless

"SACRED HEART" "SHIVERS"
Laying "NAKED IN THE RAIN"
"THIS IS YOUR LIFE"- " WILD ONE"!
Your "GOLDEN RULES" we gain

"IN DREAMS" "I SPEED AT NIGHT"
I'm "LOSING MY INSANITY"
"ANOTHER LIE": "COMPUTER GOD"
Your "HEAVEN AND HELL"- my vanity!

By "KILLING THE DRAGON"
"I COULD HAVE BEEN A DREAMER"
I'm "THE LAST IN LINE" To "SCREAM"
Like an "INVISIBLE" screamer

Now that you are gone
"THE END OF THE WORLD" is here
"STRAIGHT THROUGH THE HEART"
"PUSH" "JUST ANOTHER DAY" in fear

"CHILDREN OF THE SEA" " DYING IN AMERICA"
Is it "DEATH BY LOVE"?
"FACES IN THE WINDOW" looking for
A "GYPSY" from above

Dear "STARGAZER" from "STRANGE HIGHWAYS"
Our love "HERE'S TO YOU"
"WE ROCK" "ONE MORE FOR THE ROAD"
The "OTHER WORLD" anew

"ONE NIGHT IN THE CITY" with "NEON KNIGHTS"
"THE EYES" "STAY OUT OF MY MIND"
The "STARSTRUCK" "SUNSET SUPERMAN"
Is what we long to find

"THE MAN WHO WOULD BE KING"
Is the "INSTITUTIONAL MAN"
"SHOOT SHOOT" to "TURN TO STONE"
"WHEN A WOMAN CRIES" to plan

To "STAND UP AND SHOUT"
before " THE KING OF ROCK AND ROLL"
Though "GOD HATES HEAVY METAL"
"EAT YOUR HEART OUT" to reach the goal.

To MJ (A Tribute to Michael Jackson)

I wrote this poem in June 26th, 2009 one day after Michael Jackson passed away. I used all his hit song titles in uppercase here)

To the man who sings "THEY DON'T CARE ABOUT US"
This is a tribute from a heart grievous
You are the "MAN IN THE MIRROR" I've ever known
"YOU ROCK MY WORLD" so "YOU ARE NOT ALONE"
With your "CHILDHOOD", "THE
WAY YOU MAKE ME FEEL"
"DIRTY DIANA" "LIBERIAN GIRL " no one can kill
Cannot really kill the love in my heart
The love for your songs truly can't depart
To "HEAL THE WORLD" you precisely come along
Your "SCREAM" for "THRILLER" makes us strong
You try to "BEAT IT" all that is wrong
"WE ARE THE WORLD, WE ARE THE
CHILDREN" what a piece of song!!
You "DON'T STOP TILL YOU GET ENOUGH"
We see the "JAM" when you are getting tough
"WILL YOU BE THERE?" for "BLACK OR WHITE"?
when your urge goes always right
But trouble leads you towards the fight
Against "BAD" rumours in every night
Scandals, confusions on the ground
"DANGEROUS" "SMOOTH CRIMINAL" can never be found
""WHO IS IT?" "IN THE CLOSET?"
"REMEMBER THE TIME?"

Questions are gone with the spirit sublime
The innocent soul has "GONE TOO SOON"
No more creation of the walk of moon
Nothing will be perished, will remain ever green
I can feel "THE EARTH SONG" even "BILLIE JEAN"
You can only make me cry
More than any ghoul could ever dare try
Your songs I love to "GIVE INTO ME"
Tears for "THIS IS IT"- we could never see
Now I tell you MJ- 'God be with you!'
You'll be with us like a morning drop of dew.

A Leader's Path

He used to be a teacher of mathematics and chemistry
who was always aware of devilry's mystery
When darkness prevailed over Tanzanian soil
The vines of nation suffered blight to spoil
The fruits of hope which could have been sweeter
But the harvester called poverty made it even bitter
The branches of life became fragile by bending
He came to impose measures to curb government spending
Thus, a patriot he remains caring for each resident
He is John Magufuli, the country's fifth president
When from Cholera his countrymen were dying
He was the one saving money from flying
Away with the jubilance of the land's independence
Now humanity loves to depend on the dependence
Of peoples' dream for future on a great leaders' path
When Tanzania is blessed to attain a rebirth

28 Verses Untitled

(I)
Starry night was born to make you feel starry
But there's much more beauty within us we carry

(II)
Human in sanity must be humanity
Is sanity in vain called vanity?

(III)

Memories are aches; they are the laughter
Smiles of time flee to seize the hereafter

(IV)
Eternity is definitely a part of tomorrow
Where love will defeat the earthly sorrow

(V)
Believing is better than digesting doubt
And smile attracts more than a petulant pout

(VI)
Even a flightless bird can inspire you to fly
Don't hang yourself between 'do or die'

(VII)
When positivity is the key
You'll find peace in a cup of tea

(VIIII)
Sometimes pain in your heart can be felt very strange
Which misguides your thoughts that you fail to rearrange

(IX)
Peace is in the arms of my lover's embrace
Where this wicked world will fail to find my trace

(X)
Some pain has no relief, it can only be sealed
You can grasp the wound to feel the scar unhealed

(XI)
When sadness knows the reason of tears,
heart prepares to carry the ache for years

(xii)
I wonder at the starry pattern in the sky
Are they little pieces of moon which want to fly..?

(xiii)
I've become your heartbeat making you mine
Upon every kiss of passion our souls shine"

(xiv)
Wild waves rise and fall when they arrive
And that's what makes the calm sea alive

(xv)
Passion lingers on a state of bliss
Love loves you more when you kiss

(xvi)
Only tears can hear the sound of pain
when warm blood reddens discolored stain

(xvii)
Let the fools hold on to their treasured stupidity
Let yourself be safe in wisdom with much rapidity

(xviii)
Wounds are inspirations to make us stronger
Than the sun which blazes the day to be longer

(xix)
No food is edible, if you don't feel like eating
Standing is incredible, if you hate sitting

(xx)
Your whisper doesn't mean that you can't be loud
If you hate to nod, will you care to be bowed?

(xxi)
Sometimes the burden of love is heavier than a heavy heart
Need to carry the weight so that soul won't fall apart

(xxii)
The value of darkness can never be measured
If you don't break its cheap spell secretly treasured

(xxiii)
Seek more strength for weaker spine
No grape grows on sinner's vine

(xxiv)
It's not really outstanding when you're standing out
Outcry is the only outburst,if you can't shout

(xxv)
Future never desires to become a past
It wants to live longer while memories last

(xxvi)
Your love is not really love until you waste it
A kiss is never a kiss until you taste it

(xxvii)
When you kiss, my world falls apart
Heaven comes down to woo my heart

(xxviii)
Fidelity is wearing a mask these days
The sun cannot recognize his own rays

290 Thoughts to Ponder...

1. Many animals believe in us. Dogs, cats, all our other pets… Can we believe in ourselves? We need to learn to believe in ourselves.
2. We have no control over memories. It keeps coming back even when we desperately need it to go away.
3. Kindness is the kindest place where our hearts feel at home.
4. Don't look for anxiety in something peaceful. It will break your peace of mind into several pieces which you won't be able to mend. .
5. Wish fame could merely be a name to tame one's pride
6. Only the willingness of learning can make you learn. The person who doesn't want to learn can never learn
7. The blackness of black is so timid in front of all colours
8. We have to learn to appreciate the good qualities in our enemies
9. Life is full of letting go's…You have to let go of your parents, you have to let go of your children and in the end you have to let yourself go to the unknown world
10. The peacefulness of a lake creates a stream of passion in my heart which flows only towards my love for nature.
11. There is no way we can hold back a sinking Sun. We must wait till the next morning.
12. Only true love can read the language of a faithful heart
13. Moon mends melancholic memories
14. Rain is not all about pain and tears. Rain can smile too with its happy drops of rapture. And of course it makes the cloud go away
15. Only the clouds can tell where hidden sun-rays dwell
16. If struggle becomes your life partner, no need to divorce it. Just try to compromise and cope with its various natures.
17. It is always the troublemaker who is the trouble; but unfortunately the peacemakers are not making any peace, they are the trouble-mongers most of the time.
18. For a brokenhearted person memories are a vital part of miseries

19. Painting a black thing white won't make you stronger. Nothing false can ever last longer
20. Be prepared to face nightmares while dreaming
21. If you try to be a sage, let your modesty subside your rage
22. I always let the dream decide how to follow my future; and when it stumble, I let reality guide all those flinching steps..
23. The fire inside you can never burn you really...it is to light the best in you.
24. The empty chair in your heart should remain empty forever rather than someone unworthy sitting in there
25. While bravery conquers the heart of the brave, cowardice cries alone inside a timid
26. My imagination has no death as long as I am live...it can only imagine of being dead.
27. In the vast oceanic universe starfishes are the stars in the sky of the shore...
28. Women are flowers as they have petals. Men are funguses because their heads are all mushrooms
29. Death is always the winner in its battle with Immortality
30. Remember: the thing we fear much we carry in us...blood
31. Ocean separates lands, not souls
32. If you feel like an ordinary piece of glass, be the silver or even the mercury to make yourself a mirror
33. When we lose our voice, we can depend on simplicity's choice
34. Crossing the boundary doesn't mean crossing the limits. You can cross the boundary and still can be in your limits.
35. The misery of today can be a blessing for tomorrow. Yes, we never know- our current hardship could become a future blessing!
36. Real dreamers dream from the heart
37. Counting fingers doesn't make us mathematicians
38. Believing is better than suffering from the indigestion of doubt
39. In today's materialistic film-like-world filled with superficiality, lust seems to get all the awards in leading roles while love remains only a supporting character

40. I think poetry without metaphor is like husband and wife living in separate bedrooms
41. The land is always there…it is you who has to return
42. When memory fades, something else replaces the emptiness.. We have to find what it is… May be it's dreams or perhaps hope
43. Wild animals are less wild and more human than many humans of this world
44. The moon can never breathe, but it can take our breath away with the beauty of its cold, arid orb
45. A moment's beginning ends in a moment
46. Love is like dried flowers sometimes. Even though you watch the petals shrink and change colour, you cannot help treasuring them
47. Do not feel sad for your tears as rocks never regret the waterfalls
48. Some broken vases can still hold beautiful flowers
49. Every lake belongs to the quietness desired by the swans
50. Live alone if staying together seems lifeless
51. The easiest way to be reborn is to live and feel life everyday
52. Only the moon's smile can cure the unseen scars of darkness
53. You will never feel alone, if you run down the stairs of loneliness; as every solitary step becomes your companion
54. A lost road will remember your footsteps because someday you may want to return, tracing the way
55. Distance unites missing beats of two hearts in love
56. Patience is to wait for the ice to melt instead of breaking it
57. Love is love, even if it is illicit; like light remains light even in the darkness
58. The love of a half dead heart will keep you half alive
59. No living thing is ugly in this world. Even a tarantula considers itself beautiful
60. Even a wolf knows how to be polite when animalistic humans have no clue about politeness
61. Where in the world would a star be without the love of the sky?
62. I adore the sky wearing rainbow shawl of love for the birds so that they could fly free in warmth after the storm

63. It is the honey which makes us cruel enough to ignore the death of a bee
64. When you run out of love, it's really hard to understand whether you have lost your heart or your heart has lost you…
65. Moon is the light from a lantern in heaven
66. When reality hurts, make sure to soar above the dream-stained sky!
67. It is hard to befool a fool who has already been fooled so many times
68. Departure of a year welcomes so many new memories
69. If you allow coldness to engulf you before winter, season is helpless to help you
70. Time appears to be most wasted when someone seeks truth in lies
71. Reading books is like wearing winter clothes; it covers and warms up the body of your naked soul
72. Soft feathers cannot make a cruel bird kind
73. Spring is the fountain of love for thirsty winter
74. Distance matters only when you fail to cover it through your mind
75. A lonely soul is the best friend of itself
76. Wings are of many kinds. Butterfly's wings, vulture's wings, eagle-wings, spread wings of white swans, dragonfly's serene wings, wings of albatross, lovely wings of humming birds, tiny wings of a fly or a bumble-bee-wings; and when they fly, they fly their best according to their ability of flying. We should not underestimate the size of those heavenly wings.
77. Soul smiles through the lips of a happy face
78. Even baldness becomes a beauty of a hairless head through the heart of acceptance
79. A bird, unable to fly, is still a bird; but a human unable to love is an inexpensive stone: like a piece of uric acid stone
80. Love is such a tremendous force of feeling! When you can't stop loving, you simply cannot stop it.
81. Pets reflect you like mirrors. When you are happy, you can see your dog smiling and when you are sad, your cat cries

82. For a brokenhearted person memories are the vital parts of misery
83. Nature is the most intimate lover of mine who denudes my emotion with its intense beauty.
84. It doesn't matter how green a blade of grass is expected to be, when it's already smashed beneath the feet.
85. A strong soul reaches anyplace, anytime; body fails to restrain it. And thus, perhaps soulmates are formed
86. Water is such a lifesaver into which we cannot breathe but without taking it into us we cannot live
87. Sometimes a broken heart can mend something else's brokenness
88. Every mind should reflect to touch the green of life through trees
89. The stars will live for me, if not anything else
90. Flowers enshrine my heart between their petals; that's why my heartbeats love them so much
91. A little tranquil lake is more significant to my life than any big city in the world
92. Sharpen your life always; even though it will come to an end like a pencil, we have to keep on writing
93. Trees exhale for us so that we can inhale them to stay alive. Can we ever forget that? Let us love trees with every breath we take until we perish
94. Only pain can define the meaning of tears
95. The intriguing placidity from the slothful pace of a snail is truly very peaceful. Our world is in need of this calmness to pacify itself
96. Live to revel in just another twilight. Life may sink and disappear along with the sunset never to rise again
97. Prayer is like coffee for my soul in the morning
98. Love hurts because it holds hearts
99. Love is the name of an irrepressible moment formed inside one complete pulsation of a heart
100. Women are like locked diaries that men expect to read like open books

101. Who's gonna bring the wild animals some hope? If we don't love them the way they are..
102. We live in a world where a hut made of clay is more durable than brick buildings, because poverty doesn't allow it to be reconstructed.
103. The Sun can rise anytime in your dreams. And there night may fall anytime as well
104. Everyone writes with hand, but very few can write with heart
105. Never forget that there is a soul within you, which loves you very much,only because it's you.
106. Deep down inside we always seek for our departed loved ones
107. Too much brokenness makes things unbreakable
108. Being human doesn't make us humans. Humanity is something else only a kind and loving heart can possess
109. Dust is the parent of a star!
110. There's an infant part in our souls which longs for the lullaby truths of life every night for a tranquil slumber
111. Every past used to be a future once upon a time
112. Street children are lovely blossoms just dropped from the tree after a heavy storm. Now they need to be put together with a needle and threads of security and shelter to live into a beautiful circle of life's garland
113. Human psychology is the most mysterious thing in the world.
114. Life is one big gym where we need to constantly workout to stay fit for this world. And indeed love here is the treadmill
115. Honestly, all crows are not ravens
116. Footsteps are the wonders of staying alive to move forward
117. Facing a language you don't know is like returning to your infancy when your mother tongue used to be a foreign language to you
118. No light can cover the darkness of a liar's heart
119. Whatever the clouds plan to do; I always trust in the sun which never fails to come out
120. I feel more human when I compare the cuteness of a lizard to a newborn child's sweetness. Both are God's creations filled with precious innocence

121. My past lives alone. That's why my loneliness wants to live in the past
122. The sky has a huge heart open for all clouds even on the gloomiest of days.
123. Life is always more beautiful and worth living when you are capable of enjoying the beauty of nature
124. Don't worry about losing someone; stay careful about losing yourself.
125. The light within us can always identify our mind's darkness
126. Deceivers are the most hideous creatures in the world
127. A prisoner should know that there are thousands of imprisoned freemen living in this world…jailed in their own society, handcuffed by duties
128. Only mountains can feel the frozen warmth of the sun through snow's gentle caress on their peaks
129. To me sometimes a mute sky is more expressive than the roaring sea.
130. If you feel all damp and lonely like a mushroom, find the thick, creamy soup of joyfulness and just dive into it in order to make life tastier"
131. Love's voice reverberates with forgiveness across the room of our heart
132. Birthplace of a new year is in the heart of hope
133. We should learn to savor some moments to let time feel worth existing
134. A torpid heart in agony needs a pen to bleed
135. Old soul cries through the tears of a newborn
136. Despite its dark veins, the transparency of dragonfly's wings assures me of a pure, innocent world
137. The problem is not in the sugar when it tastes bitter, the problem is with the tongue.
138. Death's life should have listened to the moonly whispers of breathing in the coldest nights
139. A smartphone is an addictive device which traps a soul into a lifeless planet full of lives
140. A tree house, to me, is the most royal palace in the world

141. We Pisceans know how to swim without water
142. Bugs never bug my head. They are amazing. It is the activities of humans which actually bug me all the time.
143. A homeless person should know that many souls feel utterly homeless in spite of living into the bodies of wealthy homeowners
144. Love is like electricity sometimes; it may shock you anytime, yet you cannot live without it.
145. You cannot change any world unless you become a vital part of the changing.
146. Not every wall needs a ceiling
147. You cannot buy trust, you have to earn it
148. Our souls are always looking for love, and hearts wait to treasure it.
149. People don't lie to contaminate truth. They lie to pollute their hearts
150. We wait for the new year to appear to us like the hopeful sun bringing aspiring light to an eager world
151. Love comes and goes away. It is the empty heart which never leaves us.
152. Just a single cord is enough to be tangled
153. When I ache to live, my mind loves to stay with the peaceful whiteness of a pigeon's care...in boundless amity
154. Faith is the only belief which remains alive between heaven and hell.
155. Growth of human hair is the absolute blessing for a barber
156. Happiness is the most magical thing in this world the amount of which remains the same, even after distributing it amongst innumerable unhappy people.
157. A dung beetle couple in love constantly proves that you still can be in love living on shit.
158. When something means nothing to you, you can do everything you want; but someday, somehow you may have to pay for it.
159. Our regrets want to bring back many things we leave behind

160. Home was never a dream for homeless people as they used to have their homes. Living in a home was their reality. Now we need to help them to find the lost-reality again.
161. Strong anger can only make you weaker than you already are
162. Souls are flowers, only God has the right to pluck them. But those who commit suicide: their souls are the rotten blossoms of devil's garden.
163. My love for you attains immortality whenever it is touched by the thought of death
164. Unfortunately in today's world a liar seems to be more reliable than a truthful honest man.
165. My mind has a time machine; it can travel back to the past when I close my eyes and in my dreams it travels to the future.
166. Seventy years of life is nothing in front of a single day of death
167. Nothing is dark when you embosom your own light within you
168. Cyber void is so full of amazing emptiness that makes us feel fulfilled.
169. A selfie is nothing more than just an external reflection of yourself
170. Our mistakes would not wish for anything more, if we could just stop giving birth to them.
171. Written soul is called poetry
172. A gift can never be cheap or insignificant because of the heart and love it carries.
173. Milk is the only juice in a world of cows
174. Lions are neither predators nor killers. They just go for hunting like kings; because they are the kings
175. Only the writers can change or fix the past by going back to edit old works
176. The joy of knowing a foreign language is inexpressible. I find it really difficult to express such joy in my mother tongue.
177. Patience is the blue vitriol to control the fungal emotions of life
178. The real satire starts when I'm shockingly mocked, not mockingly shocked.

179. A poet can imagine an iceberg singing a melancholic song while the world leaders find it difficult to imagine proper solution to global warming.
180. I don't dream of a ceiling fan which is always here spinning above my head. I dream of a cool weather
181. The amazing face of the motherly mammal of a seal near the oceanic shore has more honesty to offer to our world than the unreliable feature of a two-faced politician.
182. That's not me. That's my duality!
183. Just a little piece of peace can cultivate the land of Palestine, but inhuman human won't let it do that....
184. Our infinitesimal hopes should survive longer than our vast disappointments
185. You can find a better you inside of you. Why don't you search for that?
186. If an infant had the capacity to think hard about this world, it would have wanted to go back to its mother's womb again
187. In the life of mathematics two plus two makes four; but in the mathematics of life two and two can make five or even three sometimes
188. Do not underestimate the muteness of a tree. The rustling leaves of it can sing with the rival wind that many of us cannot do.
189. The answer of life struggles in between two kinds of people- those who live to dream and those who dream to live. Ask them the question about death, if they can truly conceive
190. Dream is an expensive ornament to adorn your hope
191. Gym is a sacred place which makes your life feel worth existing by putting effort of care into the home of your soul called body!
192. My life is never influenced by death because I am full of resurrections after so many spiritual and emotional demises
193. You cannot taste a song but you can feel the tune relishing your heart where strings of music belong.
194. In a cruel world kindness is certainly an unsafe virtue
195. The taste of love is always amazing; even when it's bitter

196. Stop being afraid of fear, let it be scared of you
197. City life can manufacture depression with no expiry date
198. A new year never dies; it just keeps on turning into a memory. Let's help it to be a happy memory.
199. Madness is like an alternative residence. When sanity chases you out of home, take shelter in madness.
200. Never depend on a road, depend on your strides
201. Imprisoned peace sets the war free
202. An hour is indeed a long time when you count every second
203. Learn from the ants- how a tiny heart is big enough to love, help and care about another living existence.
204. Forms of love are so many. Just make sure your heart can fit in it.
205. Words inscribed in a heart can be more durable than words written on a stone
206. Needless to say that need has no limit
207. Wisdom never requires hopelessness
208. Kindness fills the vacuum of cruelty
209. Poverty's simplicity has an inexpensive beauty rooted in it, which the rich can never afford to buy
210. A hand is not enough...to never let go
211. Souls are blameless. We commit crimes inside of our mind.
212. Satan is never your well-wisher. Get the pleasure of making him annoyed on you by doing good deeds
213. The Sun is never alone as the light remains with him always. Even when he goes down sinking...sinking, the light drowns with him
214. The most disturbing sound in the world comes from the alarm clock at 5:30am
215. Never let the salt of your tears be tasteless in grief.
216. My dreams are not always with me. They can leave anytime, but I am the one who keeps on chasing them.
217. If you are a finger, your honesty is the hand to make your existence worth living.
218. Our creator is one. However you name him. Whatever you call him. He is the only one having 99 names...

219. I want to be a guileless rook to discolor the blackness of all crafty human hearts
220. Death is more meaningful than just being dead.
221. Smartphone is definitely smarter than us to be able to keep us addicted to it
222. Most of the time things against nature are scarier than the scariest things of nature
223. Every criminal has a good mind conquered by the devil
224. The amazing feeling of being alive beautifully conquers the fear of death
225. If your tears have lost the ability to hide your pain… why shedding them?
226. Symphony of peace is the murmuring sound of a river! And with the shimmering water I feel my limbs' ecstatic quiver
227. People say- 'NASA lies.' I say- 'the moon knows it all. Look at the moon and forget the spinning flat world.
228. Flight of my mind rises beneath the seagull's wings …then ocean is my motherland I feel.
229. Every dream is the beginning of a new life in your thoughts..
230. Dream hurts; yet we never stop dreaming; just like the way love hurts but we still love to love
231. There is something immaculate about loneliness which only lonely people can understand
232. Let the blue of the sky and ocean take your blue away when you feel blue
233. Love is the heart of a heart
234. Grammar is the breathing power for the life of language
235. If God sets your speed limit high, don't be afraid of your life-car being crashed.
236. Even a heart of a kitten is reliable, if you know how to rely on
237. Sharks are the lions of the sea. They glamorize the oceanic glory
238. Donate your blood from your heart to save life. Life will donate you hearts full of love, blood and contentment in return.
239. We must yield to the power of words. Even God has chosen words to communicate with his creatures like us
240. Science is theology for an atheist

241. Our miseries are inseparable, so is our every single blessing
242. Even a cockroach can be legendary by being killed by a legend.
243. Tomorrow is the only future we have. Let's live to love it!
244. Only loyal love knows the sacred path to a faithful heart
245. My words are my children. I am eternally grateful to the womb of my mind for conceiving them.
246. True love is the commitment between two souls where body never betrays
247. A heart in love is a thriller book of many stories
248. Writing fluency sometimes needs an intense agony somewhere in your mind
249. I never feel bored as long as my mind is with me
250. Smile puts a smile on all the good things in the world
251. It is always the soul and brain that really matters; never the heart or mind
252. In today's world hunger for sanity seems to be more intense than our hunger for food.
253. Let's live to believe leaving all lies behind
254. In a world of selfie-addiction smile usually is the brand name for an essential drug called pretense
255. In today's competitive world of hardship, we need to inspire each other to be inspired by each other
256. New year is the other name of a dreamful future
257. Aging is not our fault, but we certainly are guilty of feeling it.
258. Future never desires to become a past
259. A writer leads a hyphenated-life with words
260. We should not fail to hide our love for the one who fails to hide hatred
261. We have to learn to appreciate the good qualities in our enemies
262. A merciful heart beats contently stronger than many vengeful ones
263. Only righteous path leads us to the right way
264. Courage cannot be unveiled without reality
265. Love generates two kinds of tears- in pain and in ecstasy
266. Our politicians always show lame excuse to defend their cripple decisions

267. The taste of moon is like honey to all honeymooners, but after some years does the moon's scar make it bitter?"
268. Nothing is perpetual in this world. Not even your everlasting soul!
269. Bookworms are the most precious worms in the world when they are humans, feeding upon the paper's body with their starving minds.
270. We cannot prepare our fate, but we can stir it up
271. The touch of a beautiful soul with yours is the sacred beginning of love
272. A chronic poet should always be an inveterate nature-lover.
273. Reluctance devalues aptitude
274. Even a soft flicker of dream keeps us alive. We live to dream. We dream to live.
275. Let's pursue the visage of imagination
276. Some memories should be dead as they are like living corpse in mortal's bed
277. There is only one God and all atheists will learn that after their deaths
278. You have to feel to feel it. You need to know to know it better than anything else in the world. And that is love.
279. Real wealth is not the weight of coins; it is the net value of your honesty
280. Love is that indefinable moment of brokenheartedness when you cry and someone weeps with your tears
281. Politics –some verbal tics of poly-tricks
282. If you can weep with your words, the meaning of your heart can be written forever
283. We must remember that the sun is a star, but not all the stars are the sun
284. In old days, instead of asking a teacher, people looked at the dictionary to know the complete definition of teacher. Now Google becomes our teacher and to know about Google, people Google it.
285. Hope is like melted sugar, even if it changes the form, it still tastes sweet. And caramelized hope tastes even more delicious..

So, under any circumstances, we should keep on hoping for the best
286. Nature is the guardian of Africa. While the sun lights the African sky in day time, the moon begs the world to help her lighting Africa in the night
287. Every heart needs a cutting part sharper than a blade to stab agony
288. Reading is the life-saving water for our minds. Drink pure words as much as you need and remain alive!
289. Meaning of the "White House" to the war victim children of Syria or Palestine is nothing but just a white-painted house. Perhaps, they imagine Casper lives there...or maybe some dead people. They really don't have time to think about it. Because they are busy discovering their own bloody limbs along with their parents' dead bodies from the ashes of their burnt homes.

www.ingramcontent.com/pod-product-compliance
Lightning Source LLC
Chambersburg PA
CBHW022012120526
44592CB00034B/793